MW00954588

In a MIRROR DIMLY

For now we see in a mirror dimly, but then face to face; now I know in part,
but then I will know fully just as I also have been fully known.
—1 Corinthians 13:12 NASB

MICHAEL FLEMING, MD

WESTBOW
PRESS®
A DIVISION OF THOMAS NELSON
& ZONDERVAN

Copyright © 2020 Michael Fleming, MD.

All rights reserved. No part of this book may be used or reproduced by any means, graphic, electronic, or mechanical, including photocopying, recording, taping or by any information storage retrieval system without the written permission of the author except in the case of brief quotations embodied in critical articles and reviews.

This book is a work of non-fiction. Unless otherwise noted, the author and the publisher make no explicit guarantees as to the accuracy of the information contained in this book and in some cases, names of people and places have been altered to protect their privacy.

WestBow Press books may be ordered through booksellers or by contacting:

WestBow Press
A Division of Thomas Nelson & Zondervan
1663 Liberty Drive
Bloomington, IN 47403
www.westbowpress.com
1 (866) 928-1240

Because of the dynamic nature of the Internet, any web addresses or links contained in this book may have changed since publication and may no longer be valid. The views expressed in this work are solely those of the author and do not necessarily reflect the views of the publisher, and the publisher hereby disclaims any responsibility for them.

Any people depicted in stock imagery provided by Getty Images are models, and such images are being used for illustrative purposes only.
Certain stock imagery © Getty Images.

ISBN: 978-1-9736-9785-5 (sc)
ISBN: 978-1-9736-9786-2 (hc)
ISBN: 978-1-9736-9784-8 (e)

Library of Congress Control Number: 2020913073

Print information available on the last page.

WestBow Press rev. date: 08/18/2020

Scripture taken from the New King James Version® Copyright © 1982 by Thomas Nelson. Used by permission. All rights reserved.

"Scripture taken from the NEW AMERICAN STANDARD BIBLE®, Copyright © 1960,1962,1963,1968,1971,1972,1973,1975,1977,1995 by The Lockman Foundation. Used by permission. www.Lockman.org"

[Scripture quotations are] from the Revised Standard Version of the Bible, copyright © 1946, 1952, and 1971 the Division of Christian Education of the National Council of the Churches of Christ in the United States of America. Used by permission. All rights reserved.

Scripture taken from the New Century Version®. Copyright © 2005 by Thomas Nelson. Used by permission. All rights reserved.

Scripture taken from the King James Version of the Bible.

Scripture quotations taken from The Holy Bible, New International Version® NIV® Copyright © 1973 1978 1984 2011 by Biblica, Inc. TM. Used by permission. All rights reserved worldwide.

DEDICATION

This book is dedicated to the memory of my best friend, my most ardent supporter, my most insightful critic, and my love: Sally Fleming (September 30, 1942 – January 23, 2019).

INTRODUCTION

The pieces that follow are from my random thoughts and observations as I've traveled my path: an early life filled with insecurity and shame; a young adult life with too much wasted; an adult life blessed with love and family, a wife, children, and grandchildren; and now my final seasons that have been given light through God's grace. Some of these speak of morality, some are polemical, some contain a hint of humor, but all are infused with my praise and joy to the One who is in me and has given me this life on this side of heaven.

It is my greatest prayer that something here will make you reflect, contemplate, or even chuckle.

Michael Fleming, MD
April 2020

ACCLAIM FOR IN A MIRROR DIMLY

In a Mirror Dimly will encourage and help you as you walk through the various challenges of life. Dr. Fleming takes an everyday experience and uses word pictures to describe the emotions, character, and wisdom that accompany the event. You will laugh and cry as you join him on his journey. As a medical doctor, husband, father, and educator, Dr. Fleming is able to share a unique perspective that has both a cathartic and a spiritual benefit for the reader.

Dr. Fleming leads us to deal with the tender, lonely challenges of loss and separation. Yet you will never lose site of the coming victory. You will not want to put this book down. As you continue reading, you will be compelled to take Dr. Fleming's words with you as you gain a clearer picture of life's adventure. *In a Mirror Dimly* will comfort, encourage, and inspire you as you join Dr. Fleming on his life walk, pointing toward his true north.

Dr. Tom Harrison
Executive Pastor
Broadmoor Baptist Church
Shreveport, LA

CONTENTS

FOREWORD

For close to seventy years now I've been observing life—my life as well as those going on around me—with a curiosity born of a need to connect. I'm a child of the south, living in Louisiana all of my life. I grew up in a most atypical but certainly dysfunctional family. My dad spent the majority of my first fifteen years of life in prison for various white-collar crimes. My mom, my sister, and I cared for each other in those times, and I came to realize what a rock was our mother. She had graduated from college and understood the importance of education. It's not that she pushed us; it's that we recognized from a very young age that anything less than academic excellence wasn't an option.

I realized from a very early age that I wanted to be a physician. Can't say why; there were none in my family. But as a student, I was focused on that goal. I entered Louisiana State University with some scholarship help, but worked two jobs to make ends meet. I was accepted to LSU Medical School in Shreveport, Louisiana, a brand-new medical school, to be in its third graduating class. There were only forty students in that class. And it was while there that I began writing down my observations about "things." During the latter years of school, I had the opportunity to work with an amazing group of family physicians from a small community in northeast Texas. It was there that I began to know without question that I was created to be a family physician. And it was also there that I began to realize how much I liked stories and, even more, telling those stories. Besides learning to be a doctor, I collected some of my favorite stories from those years.

I began a residency in family medicine in Shreveport after graduation. I also went through a difficult divorce at the same time. After a year, I began to date this incredible lady I had met at a medical school clinic where she was volunteering. Sally was a few years older than me, but the prettiest, brightest and most compelling human I'd ever met. She had two sons from a previous marriage, I had a daughter from mine, and after a while, we decided to blend our families and become one. I adopted her two sons, bringing us closer. And then after only a year, we had our son together, completing our "his-hers-and-ours" family.

Even though I had planned to practice in the small town in northeast Texas, Sally made it clear—it's one of my favorites of these stories—that we would remain in Shreveport instead. In July of 1978, we opened the doors to my solo practice. She was a major driving force, and I depended on her advice. Over the years we added twelve family physicians to that group and built three ever-enlarging medical office buildings.

In the late 1980s, I had become involved in medical politics through one of my mentors—mentors had played and would play huge roles in my life—first, with the Louisiana Academy of Family Physicians (LAFP) and then nationally with the American Academy of Family Physicians (AAFP). I found this work heady and stimulating. In 1995, I was discovered to have a kidney cancer, quite a shock for a forty-five-year-old with a wife, four children, and a booming practice. But the experience opened my eyes more to the world around me, and I began to write more about my observations. Also, that experience helped me to understand that as King David wrote in Psalm 139:16 (NASB), "And in Your book were all written the days that were ordained for me, when as yet there was not one of them." Our time here on this side of heaven is limited, so it makes no sense to wait to do things! As I was more involved with AAFP, I decided to run for the presidency of this association of over one hundred thousand family physicians. After the election, I entered an electric three-year period of work as, first, president-elect, then president, and finally as board chair. During this time, I experienced and learned from my mentors about media. I also learned that through telling stories, I could help people understand my worldview and my observations.

I retired from my practice in 2006, far too early according to my wife. And as usual, she was right. So after I realized that I had "flunked" retirement, I accepted a job from a close friend as chief medical officer for his national home health and hospice brand. In this role I became even more convicted of the critical roles of quality and personal care for our patients. Many of my stories reflect these topics.

Over the many years, I had attended church fairly faithfully, I had read the Bible, and I could converse about my beliefs. Even though I had survived a cancer scare, I really did not have a personal relationship with God. But in 2008 at age fifty-eight, He came after me relentlessly. I later discovered in her own writings—after my wife's death—that she had been praying for this very thing for years. On a dark winter night in my home office, talking by phone to another of those mentors, I got onto my knees and surrendered my life to Christ. I haven't been the same since. And my stories reflect this.

Almost two years ago, the love of my life was found to have a brain cancer, a cruel and deadly diagnosis. For the next ten months, I marveled at her strength and her faith as she fought this beast, all the while declaring to anyone who would listen that one day soon she would be healed, either in this world or in heaven. Finally, it took her from us as she went home to be with Jesus. I miss her so, and I still grieve—not for her, because she is in paradise; I grieve for me because a part of me has been lost.

Day by day, He has opened my eyes to wonders of His creation that I'd never seen before and to mysteries in His Word that I'd never recognized before. But as one of my stories relates, now we only see "in a mirror dimly" the clarity of His creation that will astound us when we are in glory with Him. That's why I chose that phrase as a fitting title for these, my musings and observations.

Michael Fleming
January 13, 2020

ABBA, FATHER, DADDY

For you have not received a spirit of slavery leading to fear again, but you have received a spirit of adoption as sons by which we cry out, "Abba! Father!"

—Romans 8:15 (NASB)

I've talked about my complicated relationship with my father. My father died this past month, and I'm almost ashamed to say that I don't feel any different. It's complicated. Even today when my friends talk about the reverence and respect they feel for their dads, I wish I could join in the conversation. I've always seemed to have had an empty hole there. So many times as both a child and as an adult, I've wanted to just be able to put my head on his shoulder and say, "Oh, Daddy, let me tell you about …" when I fell and scraped my knee, when I suffered the changes of adolescence alone, when I had the normal disappointments and disasters. When I learned I had cancer, I wanted Daddy. At times of fear and times of rejoicing, I wanted a "daddy" there. I felt different and deprived because I missed those things. That's one of the reasons—besides the fact that I love them more deeply than I could have imagined—that I desire that loving relationship with my own children and grandchildren.

But then I found something else.

Abba is a Syriac or Chaldee word that is used several times in the New Testament. It is an intimate term for God as father. As intimate as "daddy." Now I know that I can begin my times with Him, addressing Him in this intimate way. When I'm in His presence, I'm a child wanting the love and protection of his daddy—and that's important because I never had that love and protection. So that's how I start my times with Him, sharing my fears and worries, highs and lows, and my deepest feelings with Abba.

Can you imagine that we have an invitation into His room, that we can address the Creator of the universe, the Creator of life as "daddy"? Yes. And sometimes we just need a daddy, don't we?

April 2013

Dear Mom,

I came to see you last week, but you didn't know me. You are in that final progression of dementia that has taken you away from us. But I cling to the memories of you. And every once in a while, a small window opens that reveals your personality just as it always was. A few weeks ago, I sat holding your hand while you colored in a coloring book. After a few minutes, you looked at me and said, "I know you. And I love you." No more beautiful words have I ever heard. But then you handed me a crayon, and I started coloring on the page with you. You looked at me with that old exasperated look and said, "You never could stay inside the lines."

And I couldn't! And that was the real you shining through the darkness of this evil disease for a flickering moment. How I will always treasure that small moment.

April 2014

CONSIDER NOW THE LILIES

In one of my favorite of the Psalms, King David wrote, "As for man, his days are like grass; as a flower of the field, so he flourishes" (Psalm 103:15 NASB). Just as the delicate and beautiful flowers in the field, our days will dry up and wither away.

But then Jesus clearly says to us, "Consider the lilies, how they grow: they neither toil nor spin; but I tell you, not even Solomon in all his glory clothed himself like one of these" (Luke 12:27 NKJV).

The late philosopher and writer Dallas Willard wrote, "It's the reason why God placed flowers on the earth: to have little voices calling to us constantly about grace. You walk in the field, and herse's a flower. Jesus valued the 'lilies of the field.'"[1] To our Father, we are more glorious than David's son, King Solomon, ever was. Can you imagine what that means? That flawed and imperfect as we are, we are indeed precious in His sight.

These thoughts are meant to assure us all of just that: we are His children, created in His image. And no matter how far we stray, He loves us so much that He has adorned us and clothed us to be beautiful to Him.

February 2019

WHAT I LEARNED FROM A LITTLE CHILD

But the angel said to them, "Do not be afraid; for behold, I bring you good news of great joy which will be for all the people."

—Luke 2:10 NASB

I've only been a Christian for a short time, about eight years. And in that time, I've found myself wanting to know, to understand. I think about things a lot. And I complicate things. I learned that it's not complicated, and complications distract from the true meaning. I also have found that I learn as much from children as anything. I learned about uncomplicating things from a child in Mexico.

You see, I've been blessed to be part of our church's medical mission to Mexico for the past few years. Every morning our teams—each consisting of doctors, nurses, and volunteers as well as students and faculty from the Mexican Indian Training Center (MITC)—go out to a remote church. We see all comers there: the medical staff to see after each patient's needs and our MITC partners to share the gospel.

One morning two years ago, our team had gone to a small

church in a very rural village. We had a huge turnout, and some people had to wait quite a long time to be seen. I noticed a mother with a small boy who had cerebral palsy. I truly love the children, and I have a special heart for those with CP since our granddaughter has this crippling disorder.

The MITC students led the children in singing songs of praise, and the last song they sang was "Jesus Loves Me." Soon after I saw the boy and his mother being escorted to see us, I noticed that both he and his mother were crying. I was afraid that he was in some sort of pain or distress, and I asked my friend and interpreter to ask what was wrong. Then Alejandro turned to me with his big wonderful smile and said, "Brother, those aren't tears of pain; they're tears of joy!" I asked why, and the boy replied (sorry, I can't do the Spanish), "Because Jesus loves *me*!"

In all the years that I've heard and sung that song, I've never heard the emphasis put on that word before. But for this little boy, with all of the challenges he faces, he was crying tears of joy because Jesus loves *him*. And that's the message the angel brought in Luke 2:10 (NASB). This is the "good news of great joy"—that a savior was born who would bring salvation to us all!

It's not complicated. And I learned this from a child. May all of us know that joy this and every Christmas.

December 2014

SALLY'S STORY

ON LOVE

We love, because He first loved us.

—1 John 4:19 (NASB)

Love. It's a term everyone uses far too often, I think, without really understanding what it really is and where it came from. We have been reawakened to its real truth over the past ten days. Here's what I now know.

First, most of what we hear in the movies, on television, in novels, and even from our friends is not really love. It's enchantment—things or people that make us feel good. Think of your favorite food. I'll wager that we've all said before, "I love _____!" That means we really enjoy that. No, love is reserved for much, much more important things than that.

Second, love takes at least two or more. In order to love, one has to love someone. Yes, I know you will think of someone who really seems to love themselves, but that's mere infatuation. It takes at least two. I think that's one of the reasons for a great mystery: the Trinity—Father, Son, and Holy Spirit are in an eternal communion of love; as C. S. Lewis once said, "Almost, if you will not think me irreverent, a kind of dance."[2] Their relationship, as we learn all through scripture, is one of infinite love. In fact, it seems that this is the reason He created us, flawed and helpless as we are—to love.

Next, real love requires sacrifice. Think about it. We meet someone special and fall "in love." That relationship requires each of us to put ourselves into the life of the beloved, a sacrifice. I've never heard anyone at a wedding say, "Now I'm free!" No, now they're indelibly part of the other. Mark wrote, "AND THE TWO SHALL BECOME ONE FLESH; so they are no longer two, but one flesh" (Mark 10:8 NASB). To become one flesh requires sacrifice of your individuality. All of us who are blessed to be parents know this well, don't we? Raising children requires remarkable sacrifice, but these sacrifices happen because we love our children.

Finally, back to the wonderful phrase in 1 John. Without the Trinity, without the scripture, without a loving and grace-giving God, would we know love? I don't think so. Richard Dawkins famously wrote in *The God Delusion* that humankind evolved because the strongest survived. However, if that were true, why do we all feel an innate need—a compulsion, really—to lift the downtrodden, to step in to prevent injustice or harm? Wouldn't allowing the weakest among us to die be best for our tribe? No, I'm convinced that what John wrote over twenty centuries ago remains true today. We know how to love only because He loved us first; He taught us how to love, to sacrifice, and to have mercy and grace.

Over the past two weeks, we've faced the reality of our mortality. During my wife's illness, we have been truly showered with selfless, sacrificial love—from our family, our friends, our church family and, most importantly, by the Holy Spirit. As we were informed of prayers being lifted for her, quite literally from around the world, we both felt an incredible peace envelop us. We are loved. And "we love, because He first loved us."

April 18, 2018

HE'S IN CONTROL, NOT ME

I'm having a very tough time with me, with my response to Sally's illness. As we started hospice care, I'd been more frustrated at every turn, and I needed to figure out why. A friend suggested that I was angry and that I needed to find a place for a primal scream. But the more I reflected, I'm not angry at all. I'm frustrated. And then it crystallized for me: I'm not in control here, and I don't like that. As health-care professionals, we are taught from the beginning and trained to "fix" things. We are tied up in knots when we confront somethings we can't fix. And I can't fix this!

Yesterday morning, I was able to arrange a sitter to be with her for a while so I could do some necessary errands. Driving alone has become treasured "alone" time, and I now often use that time to talk with the Lord. As I drove away from home, I let my frustrations out to him. I told Him that I was so frustrated because I can't "do" anything. After I was quiet for a bit, He whispered to me—it was a whisper, but it was as clear as though He were speaking directly into my ear—"She's in My hands." And my feelings of frustration began to ease, because it's not mine to control, and as you probably know, I don't do well with things I can't "control." But He let me know He's got this; He's in control!

It was as though a two-ton weight had been lifted. Her disease isn't improving, and her course is still unchanged, although He can do miracles. But I don't have to "be in charge!" He has her in His mighty, mighty hands, and He knows what His plans are for her. Praise God!

January 6, 2019

ON LOSING SALLY

Alfred Lord Tennyson once famously wrote, "Tis better to have loved and lost than to never have loved at all." Oh, how true.

I'm hurting now because I've lost her. But what if I'd never found her, if the Father had never joined us together. I loved the most adorable creature God ever created, and He brought us together for forty-two years. I see her everywhere I look. Every nook and cranny of my home is her: it is the way it is because that's how she wanted it. But also, every flower that she loved, the smell of her perfume, every song that was a favorite brings her and her smile to my mind. I hear her laugh. I imagine her laughing at me. I imagine her loving our grandchildren. I imagine the love on her face when she hugged one of our children. I imagine the joy on her face when she worshiped the Lord.

So, yes, I am better because I loved her. I can't fathom not having loved her, adored her, had our family with her. What a blessed man I am! But I have lost her, and I realize that my life, though forever changed, will go on. That's His will.

The coda to the eminent Victorian poet's line was penned by the equally eminent children's writer, Dr. Seuss. "Don't cry because it's over; smile because it happened."

My love, I can smile every day because I loved you.

June 7, 2019

THE TYRANNY OF UNCERTAINTY

I woke up in the middle of the night last week. What woke me was that my CPAP machine (on which I'm totally dependent) had quit working. It turned out that we had lost our electricity—and I haven't installed the generator that my wife has told me we need! Our North Carolina house in the mountains is very, very dark without electricity. I lay there awake thinking, *What will I do if I need to get up to the bathroom?* I am, after all, an aging male! I remembered the flashlight on my phone. But it was plugged into its charger in the kitchen, on the other end of the house from our bedroom. And just as I thought of this, yes, I did feel the need. Again, our house is very, very dark without electricity. I slowly and carefully made my way to the kitchen, touching walls and memorable landmarks. I actually lost my way at the end of the stair railing, and I don't know why. But I made it to the kitchen and retrieved the phone with its light.

What made all of this so frightening? Was it the darkness? I don't think so. Remember: darkness is really not a "thing." It is, instead, the absence of something, the absence of light. And without light, I was uncertain—uncertain about where I was, where I was headed, and where I was going. Sound familiar?

Right now we're going through one of those difficult times. Cancer is a scary diagnosis, and we're in the midst of all of the therapy that is available. The Lord told us we would have these challenges in our lives. But the one thing that we are not is uncertain. Sally has said since the diagnosis was made that she is absolutely *certain* that she will be healed, one way or the other. Because she knows His promise to us, that with Him we will have eternal life.

On our own, our entire life trajectory is uncertain, isn't it? On our own, we spend our lives trying to navigate, trying to find our way through a dark space full of potential dangers, perils, and hazards. But, bring light into the room, and suddenly, we can see! Bringing light into the darkness gives us certainty in an uncertain world.

That's why we need light, isn't it? And what did Jesus say? "Then Jesus again spoke to them, saying, 'I am the Light of the world; he who follows Me will not walk in the darkness, but will have the Light of life'" (John 8:12 NASB).

He will bring certainty to a world that is, by itself uncertain. And that is all that we need!

July 29, 2018

YOU CALLED HER MOM

To my children and grandchildren:

> The Lord said to Moses, "I will also do this thing of which you have spoken; for you have found favor in My sight and *I have known you by name*."

> —Exodus 33:17 NASB

> Behold, I have *inscribed you* on the palms of My hands; Your walls are continually before Me.

> —Isaiah 49:16 NASB

How we identify each other is supremely important; it succinctly identifies in what esteem the user holds the identified, and with what level of intimacy. And certain names rank far above all others in the pantheon of names. One of those at the highest level is "Mom."

I knew and loved her as Sally—in more official reports as Sara, but mostly as Sally. And I am so emotionally connected to that name that it is painful. Anytime I hear this name spoken, from across the room or on television, my mind sees her as she was, beautiful, gracious, and loving me. We called each other pet names, as couples do. But I knew her as Sally.

I was never able to know her as "Mom." And how I envy you that you did. For all of us, possibly the most important human relationship we'll ever experience is with our Mom. After all, she tolerated you for nine months of discomfort, nausea, and sleepless nights only to then go through the pains of childbirth. Even after all of that, she loved and cherished you. She wept with joy at your first words and cheered your first step. She comforted when you had a hurt, and she rocked you to sleep and loved you no matter how tired she was. As you matured, she prayed for your protection, your growth, and your success. Most of all, she prayed for you to know the Lord—I have proof of her prayers in her notes. But you were special, because you called her Mom.

And then came our grandchildren, one by one, much anticipated and precious. She held each of you in her arms and in her heart. You knew her as Grandmother, and she delighted in that name.

Her parents named her Sally. But only God can bless us with the name Mom/Grandmother.

May each of you live your life blessed by the blessings of her. And may you love yours as she loved you.

Dad
April 16, 2019

HER WORDS, HIS PLAN

Since Sally's death my family and friends and I celebrate her by the telling and retelling of "Sally stories." This is one of my absolute favorites, and it portrays the very essence of the strong woman I married.

We had only started dating. Both of us had been through divorces and were a bit wary. She had two young sons, and I had a daughter. I was an intern with little to my name more than the scrubs and white coats I wore to work every day. I spent many weekends working in a small northeast Texas town, Linden. The group of doctors there had spoken of me joining their successful practice after finishing my residency, and I thought that's where I would end up.

I didn't know how serious this budding relationship was. I invited her to come over to Linden one Saturday while I was working there. We took a drive for me to show her around town—it took only ten minutes! We drove back to the apartment where I stayed. She got into her car and backed out of the parking area. Then suddenly, her car stopped, and she pulled up to where I was standing. She rolled down the window, looked up at me with the look we would all come to know that meant that the following words were serious and nonnegotiable, and said, "I just need you to know that my children are not growing up in Linden, Texas!" And then she rolled up her window and drove away.

So I learned two important things that day: first, it was getting serious; and second, I would not be practicing in east Texas. I also have come to understand that He had a plan for our life together, a life together filled with children, grandchildren, our church, travel, a successful practice, and lots of love. What a blessed man I am!

January 2020

THE BELL

An excellent wife who can find? Her worth is far above jewels. The heart of her husband trusts in her, and he will have no lack of gain. She does him good, and not harm, all the days of her life.

—Proverbs 31:10–12 NASB

Her children rise up and bless her; her husband also, and he praises her…

—Proverbs 31:28 NASB

To our family, Sally was our rock. She was a godly woman who loved me and her children absolutely and unconditionally. She was the definition of "an excellent wife." However, she was very plainspoken. It was frequently said of her, "If you don't want to hear her real opinion, don't ask!"

The first quarter of 1995 started with pain for her and then progressively worsened. In late January, Sally's mother, Beth, died suddenly and unexpectedly. She increased the time she spent with her dad, Bennie, and we soon understood that he was showing early signs of the Alzheimer's disease that would take him. The first few months were so difficult for her. And then …

I was admitted to the hospital for an acute illness, but while there, it was discovered that I had a large mass on my left kidney—a cancer. On the ides of March 1995, not yet three months from her mother's death, her husband had major surgery to remove the cancerous kidney.

Now I will openly admit that I don't do pain well and that Sally was about as stoic as anyone could find (in her entire ten-month journey with brain cancer, she never, ever complained of pain). So after discharge from the hospital, she brought into our bedroom a bell so that she could hear me when I needed her.

I really don't think that I overused that bell; however, I had been home only about three hours when she took the bell away from me! It was not that I rang it too often. It was that I rang it "too aggressively."

In the years since then, I have looked high and low for that bell, but I never saw it again. When my children came to help me clean out the house after her death, I asked them to look for it.

The bell is gone. I suspect that she got rid of that same day that she took it from me. She called it "tough love"!

April 2019

FAMILY

SHADOWS AND GRANDSONS

For the Law, since it has only a shadow of the good things to come and not the very form of things, can never, by the same sacrifices which they offer continually year by year, make perfect those who draw near.

—Hebrews 10:1 NASB

I have a fascination with the scriptural concepts of darkness and light. The apostle John said it best: "The Light shines in the darkness, and the darkness did not comprehend it" (John 1:5 NASB).

I also am fascinated by the wisdom of the very young, a wisdom that can only be a gift from the Father, because they are too young to understand the depth of their thoughts. I was playing with my three-year-old grandson, John, on the driveway one beautiful, sunny fall day. He was riding his tricycle—fast, as usual. He ran across my shadow, and I laughed and said, "John, you ran over Granddaddy!" He looked up at me, somewhat perplexed, and replied, "But, Granddaddy, that's not you. It's just your shadow!"

In his innocent wisdom, he knew. He knew that shadows aren't real objects, only an image from a background of light.

We are given this wonderful image by the writer of Hebrews. The shadows of legalism and "Phariseeism" aren't real; they are only images of the old objects. And the new, our salvation that is promised to us, is the light that illuminates them. A new light reflecting our new promise, given for all time to those who believe. But still we go on, tilting at shadows, worrying about this and that.

We, too often, allow those shadows to stir up our fears and insecurities. When all along, He told us that He had done away with all of those things, that His light has illuminated our shadows, and "in Him, there is no darkness at all!" (1 John 1:5 NASB). And he has promised that as the good shepherd, He "leads me through the valley of the shadow of death" (Psalm 23:4 NASB).

I've no doubt that's what grandson John meant: Granddaddies are really dumb!

October 18, 2015

NO. 7

We're back here in Nashville, and I'm sitting with my new grandson, Graham, our seventh, while Sally takes Sarah Ann for an outing away from the house for a bit. I took John, the two-year old, to school this morning, and we sang loudly together all the way! I take him in Sarah Ann's car since the car seat is there. She has a CD of Sunday school songs that he loves, and we sang "He's Got the Whole World in His Hands" about ten times. He sings so joyously, how could anyone not understand that this is an absolute reflection of God's glory!

Graham is sleeping in my arms as I one-hand type this. How blessed we are! Something makes me think that one day many years hence he'll be holding his grandson and telling him how much he loves him just as I am doing now.

June 2016

LINDEN STORIES

CANDLES

I was working in Linden for the doctors of the Glenn-Garrett Clinic over the week between Christmas and New Year's 1976. The doctors had all gone away for a ski vacation, and I was there feeling very alone as a very "green" resident. A call came to the emergency room at the hospital requesting a house call for a dying patient who lived far out in the surrounding countryside, in fact, so far out that the ER nurse had called the local deputy sheriff to take me out there.

We arrived at the large, old farmhouse in the dark of the late December night. All of the family was there with the elderly man I found propped up on pillows in his bed struggling for breath. The room was large and dark, and there were candles in the window— how well I remember those candles! The deputy and I approached the bedside and I began my assessment. It was clear that he was struggling with heart failure and was in acute pulmonary edema, fluid filling his lungs, preventing him from breathing. I drooped his right arm off the bed and prepared to give him an intravenous injection of a strong diuretic to relieve the fluid.

Despite the chill of the December night, I was shivering from "performance anxiety" as I located a vein and began to "push" the medicine. About midinjection, he gave a deep, breathy sigh, and he expired. All I could do was to drop my head and pray, when from the back of that room one of the family members in an east Texas drawl that can't be heard anywhere else summed it all up; he said, "Shore killed him quick, didn't it!" I was afraid to move. They didn't still lynch people out here, did they?

But that wasn't it. The family were appreciative, and they recognized that this was the end of a fruitful, well-lived life. The deputy came over and put his hand on my shoulder and said softly, "Let's go, son."

A week later, I received a letter from the man's daughter expressing the family's appreciation. And I learned a lesson that would stay with me forever: death is an inevitable point on the continuum of life.

But I did have nightmares about pushing IV diuretics.

December 2002

THE LIVING ROOM OF THEIR LIVES

My career, indeed, my life, was fashioned after those who took the time to mentor. Not having a full-time father, I always looked to others for a role model to be followed. One of the most important of all to me was Dr. Vernon Glenn, a matchless primary care physician who practiced in a small town in northeast Texas. He was an icon not just to me but to an entire community who loved him for his care, his ethic and for his loving heart. Not that he couldn't be gruff—I learned that quickly! But when he spoke, the words were worth hearing.

One afternoon, we were traveling together in his pickup on the dusty roads of northeast Texas in the summertime. I was reflecting with wonder over our day so far and wondering aloud about the patient we were heading out to see. That morning, I had helped Dr. Glenn with the delivery of a new life, the baby son of the town banker. Then Dr. Glenn told me that we were on the way out to see an old friend of his, a farmer/rancher who was dying. In fact, he was driving too fast on that dirt road, but he wanted us to be there in time.

I asked why that was important. He immediately jerked the wheel of that pickup over to the shoulder, and we skidded to a sudden stop. He looked over to me and spoke words that shaped the way I wanted to spend my life caring for people; he said to me, "Boy! The greatest compliment anyone can ever give us is to be invited to their coming into this world or their time of leaving this world. Don't ever forget this! These folks invite us into the living room of their lives. Always honor that trust."

What a statement! What a charge! Indeed, that's what we as primary care physicians do, and for that, and for Dr. Glenn, I am eternally grateful.

January 8, 2020

JACK AND RABY

These were a most interesting couple, well known around Linden. Jack was the town grave digger. The first time I met them, they were walking down the hall in the clinic, Jack walking ahead and Raby following as she always did. I asked if I could help them. Jack replied, "Show him, woman!" She reached down to the hem of the muumuu she always wore and pulled up over her belly. She had spilled a pan of hot grease down her abdomen. I took care of them that day, and we became odd friends.

I was working in the emergency department at the Linden hospital over a long holiday weekend. The call came in that the ambulance was on the way in bringing Jack for emergency care. It seems that someone else was in the cemetery working on a grave, Jack became upset because that was his job, and the two got into a fight—not an uncommon occurrence for Jack. The other combatant had a shovel and swung it at Jack's head, making solid contact in the right frontal area of Jack's scalp. When he arrived at the emergency room and I looked into the wound, I was looking through a crease in his skull down to gray matter—his brain!

The closest neurosurgeon was at the medical school in Shreveport, my school. Finally getting him on the phone on this weekend day, he advised me to irrigate and clean the wound, put in some sutures to close the skin over the skull wound, and then transfer him as soon as possible to Shreveport.

Jack had major neurosurgery and recovered well. I didn't see them again for several months. One day, I was working in the clinic there, and Raby came in. I asked her how Jack was doing. Very seriously, she replied, "You know, since Jack had his surgery, he's gotten so much nicer to me, and he don't beat me no more!"

Couldn't make this one up.

April 2015

MUSINGS

GIVERS AND TAKERS

The leech has two daughters, "Give," "Give."

—Proverbs 30:15 (NASB)

I have come to believe in the notion that there are clearly two distinct groups in the world: givers and takers. The vast majority of givers don't possess a lot. They are of modest means. According to research on philanthropy, when givers give of their resources, they tend to give to many different things: their churches, charities, the needy, and to small groups that touch their hearts. And many of these gifts are anonymous, never meant to be known. When takers do give of their resources, they expect recognition. But takers don't like to give, because they believe they are owed.

Givers give of more than just their resources. They give their time, their energy, and their hearts. Takers are like a vacuum in space, sucking up time and energy. Nothing causes fatigue like being close to a taker.

Givers are open and caring. They ask how you are, because they really want to know. Takers keep their feelings closed, and almost any relationship requires work.

Givers don't "give until it hurts." In fact, they give until it feels good. Takers take until they feel they have gotten what's due to them. But they somehow never do.

Givers understand that the most important meaning to any gift is to the giver, not the receiver. Takers take, believing that anything given to them is somehow deserved, that they are entitled.

Being a giver or a taker isn't defined by age, race, gender, or heredity. It is instead defined by a worldview, a belief that there is something far greater than themselves that promises to give back. Takers can become givers; in fact, reformed takers are some of the most committed and prolific givers one could find. But givers rarely regress to takers.

Givers work to be able to give. Takers finagle to find ways to take more and more. And as Thomas Jefferson so famously opined, "The democracy will cease to exist when you take away from those who are willing to work and give to those who would not."

Anything sound familiar?

December 5, 2012

AIN'T NOBODY'S FAULT BUT MINE

Last weekend, we attended a benefit concert for the local free clinics here in Hendersonville, our getaway place in the beautiful mountains of western North Carolina. We were entertained by a Swiss group, The Kruger Brothers, who now call the mountains of North Carolina home. One of the songs they performed keeps coming back into my head as I watch the news coverage of the terrible tragedy that Hurricane Katrina has wrought on the Mississippi and Louisiana gulf coasts: the title, "Ain't Nobody's Fault but Mine." Mother Nature in her annual show of unconfined and unabashed fury has, again, wrought havoc with all of the best plans of men. I wonder who we'll find to blame for all this? Who can we sue to "get what is mine, what belongs to me!" (I just heard that exact line in a television advertisement for a local law firm).

It would seem when reading the news or watching the television news or even looking at the cover of a telephone book that anything that happens must be someone's fault and someone should pay. In fact, most things that happen me, to quote the line from The Kruger Brothers' song, "Ain't nobody's fault but mine."

If I were to continue to smoke, to ignore the evidence that is now accepted by the world of medicine that tobacco kills, and should I then develop lung cancer or have a heart attack, "Ain't nobody's fault but mine." If I am unfortunate enough to spill hot coffee in my lap and I am burned because the coffee was, well, hot! "Ain't nobody's fault but mine!" If I were to be dumb enough to drink until I slobber and then get into my car to drive and have an accident that causes much pain and suffering, "Aint't nobody's fault but mine!"

But now that we have a national mind-set that whatever befalls me must be someone else's fault, who can we blame? This obviously presents a serious moral question for those who would believe such garbage, right?

Oh well. Ain't nobody's fault but mine!

August 30, 2005

THE TWENTY-EIGHTH AMENDMENT TO THE CONSTITUTION OF THE UNITED STATES

Is anyone happy about what's happening in Washington these days? No one that I know. Over the past few years, the buffoonery of our elected has affected all of us, so it seems that it's time for the people to demand some accountability. Well, that's the job of elections, you say. But, you see, that won't happen: because those who only "get" won't vote for those not interested in giving.

Therefore *[fanfare and flourish here]*, I propose the Twenty-Eighth Amendment to the Constitution of the United States.

"But they don't uphold the current Constitution," you say. And you're right! That's why I call this Twenty-Eighth Amendment the "Civics Amendment." It would have three parts, each distinct, but each requiring our elected representatives to do some things that for our entire history would have seemed obvious.

Amendment 28, Article 1, would require that any part of any bill considered by either house be germane to the topic of the bill. Actually, this requirement for being relevant is part of normal parliamentary procedure, but Congress never met a rule it didn't couldn't break! This would mean no more funds for a congressman's pet local project attached to foreign aid bills, and no more foreign aid handouts slipped into energy bills. It means that if the bill is filed for one thing, anything attached to that bill must be about that topic. No exceptions.

Amendment 28, Article 2, would require that any member of Congress who wishes to vote on any bill before either the House or the Senate must, before they are allowed to cast a vote, score no less than 80 percent on a quiz about the content of that bill. No staff. Only members. They can take it as many times as it takes to pass it, but at least they would have some idea of what's in the bill. Had this been in place for the Affordable Care Act (ObamaCare) the vote might have been three to two!

Amendment 28, Article 3, would require that any citizen who wishes to run for and serve in an elected office must pass a high school civics class. That would mean that they would have some knowledge of the Constitution—all of it, not just the parts they want to use. They would be reminded that the crafters of our Constitution separated the powers among three branches of the federal government: a legislature, the Congress—with the power "to make all laws which shall be necessary and proper for carrying into execution the foregoing powers, and all other powers vested by this Constitution in the government of the United States, or in any department or officer thereof" (Article I, Section 8); an executive branch led by the president, charged to carry out these laws (nowhere is this branch given authority to make laws!); and a federal judiciary headed by the Supreme Court, granted the authority to interpret and apply the law (Article III, Section 1).

And finally, all of them must publicly declare in voice and on paper that they understand and agree that all three of these branches derive their power from the people—it seems that they need reminding.

April 2013

AMERICA IS GREAT BECAUSE AMERICA IS GOOD

America is great because she is good. If America ceases to be good, America will cease to be great.

—Alexis de Tocqueville

Why is America different? Is there such a thing as "American exceptionalism"? We are, indeed, different; and yes, we are also exceptional. Why is that? There is one remarkable thing that has defined us from our beginning: unlike any other nation ever on the face of the planet, our Declaration of Independence asserts that the rights—life, liberty, and the pursuit of happiness—of our citizens are not rights granted by a sovereign power, a ruler, or a king. They are instead rights with which every man is born as gifts of an almighty God. And our Constitution—the declarative statement by which we live—brings forth an outline of these freedoms. And these freedoms set forth by our founders as "ordained by God." I believe that this inborn recognition leads us to one of the most unique of all American characteristics: philanthropy. The word means "love of humanity," and on so many levels, this is uniquely

American. What happens when there is a natural disaster on the other side of the globe? Americans are the first on the scene, with millions of dollars of aid, and even more importantly, with "boots on the ground." Since the Marshall Plan after WWII, Americans have even aided nations against whom we fought.

You see, with our freedom as a gift from God, we understand that this also brings responsibility. We believe that it is our responsibility to "care for the widow and the orphan," as the Bible so often exhorts. And it is our responsibility to care for those not as fortunate as we are.

But why is this not so in other nations? It all has to do with from where we derive our freedoms. If freedoms are granted from ourselves, then we ought to care for ourselves. But when freedoms and rights are expressly granted by governments, then the people will expect the government to respond, not themselves.

A free people ruled by the will of God will act differently. We will give to churches, organizations, and others that support what we believe. We will give for the welfare of others. A people ruled by other people will sit back and expect the rulers to act. And act governments will. But let me ask, have you found one example where government can do anything as efficiently as people can? Have you ever seen any government program the ends or expires when the work is done? Name for me a tax that has actually expired, despite what its enacting legislation might have said?

There are a handful of things that have uniquely characterized the grand experiment that is America. De Tocqueville was prescient in his comment, and our being "good" pretty much encapsulates this uniqueness. But we must take to heart the latter part of his comment. When we quit being good, we will no longer be great. When we depend on a government to meet our needs, we will subsist in subservience to rulers who rule for their own good.

Let us remain good, to remain great.

November 2015

THE COLORS OF THE YEAR

For some reason, I'm reminded of the seasons of the year not by the temperature but by the colors. It seems more vivid to me now, but that may be because I didn't take the time to look so closely before.

Without a doubt, spring is my favorite, and spring is green. As I walk through our neighborhood or the golf course, what always amazes me most are the many colors of green I can see: the rich, dark green of emerging grass; the bright colors of the elms and pecan that contrast with the deeper green of the magnolias and pines, and in my part of the world, the gossamer clouds of pine pollen that appear yellow-green against the blue sky. The tiny green leaves give way to the gaudy pinks and purples and whites of the azaleas. Yep, spring is definitely green.

Summer is blue. Blue sky, blue water. The slate blue of a summer dawn, followed by the blazing blue sky of the midday. Ending in the palette of blue with yellow and orange highlights at the setting of the sun. In the summer even green appears blue. The walls of rhododendron and mountain laurel take on such a deep, verdant color that you would swear they were painted on a canvas instead of being real enough to touch. Blue is luxurious like a summer day.

Autumn, my second favorite. From the deck of our home in the mountains of western North Carolina, I can see an entire spectrum of yellows and oranges and reds and occasionally purples that appear pasted on a collage. But here, autumn is orange, giving meaning to the term *crisp*. There is a smell of change in the air as all the colors become even more vibrant.

Winter. Ah, gray winter. The gray smoke that swirls from the chimneys that warm the winter nights. Even on a sunny day, the ghosts of the trees are gray and lifeless. The wind-driven surface of the lakes reflects the gray winter sky, and grayness is all around.

March 20, 2007

POLITICALLY CORRECT VS. RIGHT

Moral relativism is a philosophy that asserts there is no global, absolute moral law that applies to all people, all of the time, and in all places. Instead, it espouses a view best defined by Nietzsche, who wrote, "You have your way. I have my way. As for the right way, the correct way, and the only way, it does not exist." Hmm. I don't buy that, do you? If this were to be true, then why do we all know that certain things (e.g., murder, genocide, and the like) are wrong? Where did that innate knowledge come from? I can answer that, although the relativists would strongly disagree and say that my belief in the Bible is "intolerant" of other beliefs. But then who says that their beliefs aren't intolerant of mine?

Our national problem is that we've become consumed by the idea of political correctness. According to the Merriam-Webster dictionary, *politically correct* means agreeing with the idea that people should be careful to not use language or behave in a way that could offend a particular group of people. It's a notion that seems to have been co-opted by the self-described "progressive tolerance police." But I think if any reasonable person really considers things, the concept that they propose isn't politically correct at all. It's all relative.

You see, if anyone demands that all language or behavior be such that does not offend a particular person or group of people, then who decides what might offend whom? Who or what is the authority? Are these folks who have screamed loudest concerned that much of their behavior and language is offensive to me? Anytime anyone stands for anything that depends on how anyone *feels*, what they are demanding is relative—it's only offensive if *I* think it's offensive. That's moral relativism. In fact, wasn't it this kind of moral relativism that led to the Holocaust? Shocking, eh? But it was, wasn't it? When the leaders of Nazi Germany made amoral anti-Semitism the "politically correct" norm, it wasn't a big step. Some have called it the tyranny of the majority, but I call it the tragedy of lost souls that is relativism.

So to paraphrase the question heard on every playground every day, "Says who?" And to answer, I'd suggest that even though they would strongly protest the answer, there is a well-recognized moral "right" as opposed to a moral "wrong." We all know "right" from "wrong," but how do we know this and where did this knowledge come from. It's from scripture. That's right all you politically correct folk, the Bible. I'd challenge anyone to show me where else it might have originated. I can hear the blogosphere churning now to answer, but ask yourself this question: Is there anyone in the world right now doing something that you feel is morally wrong? Of course, there is. But now ask yourself: Why is that wrong?

Is it wrong just because I think it's wrong? You'll most probably answer something like, "Because it just is." I ask again, "Says who?" There's only one answer. And it's not relative.

May I suggest that we remove the concept of political correctness from our culture? And replace it with an authoritative "right" from the one soul of righteousness.

June 2015

LINES AND CIRCLES

Since I travel a great deal by air, and since I love to fly, I've had a lot of time to survey the earth from above and think. Today, I'm comfortable at 39,000 feet looking down on the beautiful western United States. Mountains and canyons are divided by valleys that are carved into squares and circles of irrigated fields. My eyes are drawn to the shapes I can see below, and something about these shapes fascinates me. You see, it's easy to tell the difference between natural shapes and man-made ones: there are no straight lines or circles in nature; straight lines only appear in what man has made.

The ridges and hills appear as folds and creases in a rocky blanket with angles on angles on angles. Small lakes are defined by irregular shorelines that follow the topography. Forests are a plush carpet of irregular depth, no pattern or heft discernible. And valleys, flat as an iron, meander through rifts in the crags and spires of the mountain peaks.

But roads, ribbons of concrete, asphalt, gravel, and now dirt divide the landscape into perfect squares and triangles. There are occasional offsets and curves, but straight for the most part. It's easy to pick the roads from the streambeds, one straight and uniform, the other winding and uneven. Fields are mostly perfect squares and rectangles except in the plains, where perfect circles of crops appear as if traced by a giant compass.

It seems man yearns to construct an orderly vision. We build with plumb lines and protractors, imperfect creatures striving to build perfection. But God created us all irregularly, not very even, not all the same, with angles and unevenness, but nevertheless perfect. And He has set before us His divine "plumb line." How wonderful the difference!

August 2008

THE "ETERNAL FLAME"

It had been a terrible week! I felt sorry for myself and what I'd been put through. I was in a car with a driver on the way from my hotel to the airport at 5:00 a.m. after having been in that hotel room for less than eight hours after a grueling travel day after an evening speech after a grueling week away from home. And now I was to meet my CEO to fly back to where I had already been and then back to New Orleans for a noon talk. Wasn't I worth more than this? Wasn't I a health care executive with important places to be and movers and shakers to influence? Wasn't I the guest professor and speaker at these events? Wasn't I a professional who deserved more?

I-10 in New Orleans passes directly by one of the cemeteries there with ornate above-the-ground vaults and memorials, all built in remembrance of those gone to their ultimate reward, whatever that might be. And then I saw it in the early morning bleakness: From one of the most ornate of the tombs came the flickering tongues of what was surely meant to be the "eternal flame," a memorial of one loved and lost to remember the greatness indicated by that monument.

Who was this person remembered in this way? A father, a grandfather, a husband? A loving mother, grandmother, wife, a matriarch? A civic giant who had changed the course of this city's history? A beloved teacher, a writer of extraordinary talent? A mentor? A friend? Now only a flickering flame visible from an interstate highway to commuters hurrying between here and there. How we long for immortality; and how fleeting a concept.

What is eternal? If it is to be remembered forever, how fleeting! Ask 100 high school seniors for whom the eternal flame in Arlington National Cemetery is intended to remember, and what response would you receive? Who was John Kennedy? Ask them who was Gandhi or Churchill. In fact, we—all of us—are visitors to this tiny, insignificant planet for only a moment in the grand unknown that is time. We are visitors here, never meant to tarry long or feel at home.

Eternal only exists in the mind of God. It is only possible to understand in the context of an almighty, omnipotent Father. As the wise Solomon wrote, "He has made everything beautiful in its time. He has also set eternity in the hearts of men; yet they cannot fathom what God has done from beginning to end" (Ecclesiastes 3:11 NASB).

So our only way of understanding "eternal" is to know God. Our "eternal flame" is the light that John describes (1 John 1 NASB). Let us move not toward the myth of earthly immortality, but toward the true eternal light.

All flesh is grass, and all its beauty is like the flower of the field.

—Isaiah 40:6 RSV

The grass withers, the flower fades, but the word of our God will stand for ever.

—Isaiah. 40:8 RSV

May 2015

THE GIFT

We are just returning from a trip to Wyoming. Every morning, I walked outside our hotel marveling at the splendor of the peaks of the Grand Tetons and the unbelievable beauty that our God has created for us. And then it struck me how much a metaphor is this grandeur for the grace that He so willingly gives.

You see, some who live and work within view of these vistas begin to take this beauty for granted. Just as I do with the beauty of the green trees and grass, and multicolored blossoms around our Louisiana home. Every day I walk and drive through this beauty, but rarely do I acknowledge how truly incredible the green of the pine trees contrasts with the dark green oaks, and with the bright green of the lawn grass.

So to accept the beauty of God's creation, I must acknowledge them. I don't deserve them. How could I deserve the majesty of a mountain peak or the intricate beauty of a lily?

But God has put them on His earth for one thing. For us. Because He loves us.

And His grace, His saving grace, is ours. Because He loves us.

David says, in Psalm 18:19, "Because He delights in me, He

saved me" (NCV). His salvation is for us to share. But it is only ours if we accept it.

Gifts are like that. What is a gift worth if unopened? If you gave me a gift and I put it in a closet and never opened it, never accepted it, how much is it worth to me? And His grace is His gift, no different than the mountain peaks that I so admired. If I don't look upon them and appreciate their beauty, they are of no value.

How great is our God?

July 2010

THE OPEN SHADE

For over thirty years, our neighbors lived across the street from us. Lois Anne and John were a retired couple. I was honored to care for them for twenty-eight years through serious injuries and chronic diseases. Lois Anne was the prim and proper definition of the southern lady, a military wife who had raised two children during John's tours as an Army colonel. She was gracious and kind and always proper. Then a severe brain injury caused a complete personality change.

The ramrod straight colonel cared for our entire neighborhood as the handyman. His business cards read "Every Woman's Favorite Husband." John could build, craft, or repair anything. He was crusty and tough, but we got along even though he was never quite comfortable that I wasn't military.

John had severe COPD and couldn't sleep many nights. I could see the upstairs window of his room from our kitchen, and many early mornings, I saw a single light from their house, shining through an open shade. John would be at his computer, working on some new idea. Somehow, seeing that light through the open shade every morning reassured me that all was well.

Then, Lois Anne died suddenly. After her death John's disease progressed rather rapidly, and he did little to prevent that, smoking many packs a day as he had since his tours in war zones. Before very long, he couldn't get to his computer, and the shade was closed. Hospice care and his caretakers provided for his needs. But the shade stayed closed.

Early one morning, another neighbor called and told me that John had died early that morning. As I walked across our street, I looked up at his room, and as much as I grieved for John, I grieved for my loss—the loss of a friend, a patriot, and the loss of the reassurance of the open shade.

Their children sold the house, and now a new family has moved in. This morning as I made coffee, habit made me look again across to that upstairs window. And it was open and a light shone through.

And so again, the light in the window goes on. Life goes on. But we do not. God has reminded me that this isn't our home; we're just passing through.

March 2015

THE POLARIZING LENS

It's a balmy January 2 here in North Louisiana. On New Year's Day, the temperature bumped up against eighty degrees here. Today's a work holiday, so I slept in a bit this morning, going out for my morning walk at about 9:00 a.m. instead of the usual 6:00. The sky was bright, and I remembered my new sunglasses, so I circled back and got them from my car.

As I set out, I marveled at the intense blue of the morning sky and the lush greens of the pines and live oaks that populate our part of the world. It had been quite a while since I had seen the world at this time of the day through polarized lens. You see, it's been a while since I've had polarized sunglasses that matched my prescription for my dwindling eyesight—maturity, you know. As I walked farther, I began to notice the details a bit more—the variegated colors of the leaves on the ground, the almost iridescent sheen of the silky cocoons that still clung to twigs and braches long blown from their homes by the recent winds, the way some parts absorbed while others reflected the different waves of light energy. When viewed without the polarized lens, these patterns of nature disappeared, drab and invisible to the human spectrum.

How much like the way our individual personalities color our own perceptions of reality. When faced with any challenge, some view all the negative potentials and dangerous wave patterns; others are able to assess dispassionately and see positives and negatives; and still a few recognize that although there may be untoward effects of the challenge, every challenge represents opportunity.

I believe that our paths through life are a consequence of the choices we make at every fork in the road. How we assess each option is a factor of which set of polarizing lenses we choose to use. Usually, whether in our relationships, our jobs, parenting, or almost any form of human interaction, we get whatever we expect to see through our lens: Expect little—from our marriages, our children, our lives—and little is almost certainly what we'll get; expect much—have our positive polarizers on!—and much we will be destined to receive.

January 2, 2006

IN HIS WORD

IN A MIRROR DIMLY

For now we see in a mirror dimly, but then face to face; now I know in part, but then I will know fully just as I also have been fully known.[1]

—1 Corinthians 13:12 NASB

Last year, I had cataract surgery. The morning after my first procedure, I walked outside to retrieve my newspaper—yes, we older folks still get a newspaper—and I was astounded at how beautifully clear and bright were the colors of that December morning. It was a brightness that I had not appreciated in many years because of the clouding of my lens. And then …

I returned to Cordoba, Mexico, last week for our church's annual medical mission trip. I have fallen in love with these people, and I marvel at their faith. I also am enamored of the beauty of this mountainous area, particularly Pico de Orizaba, the highest mountain in Mexico and the third highest in North America. It rises almost solitary from a lower mountain zone, its snow-covered caldera giving proof its origin as a volcano. How splendid is God's creation!

Our group breakfasts in a small hotel in Fortin. There are

beautifully clear windows that look directly out at the peak; however, my seat at the table was facing away from the peak. Then I noticed it: a mirror directly in front of me reflected the glorious view. How majestic it was on this clear morning!

Then I remembered the apostle Paul's words in 1 Corinthians. "For now we see in a mirror dimly" (1 Cor 13:12 NASB). Yes, more dimly than I could see with my cataracts. But even now I am amazed at the glory of His creation. Can you imagine what it will be like to see His works clearly? Without the corrupting haze of our sinful nature? Without the tarnish of the world around us?

We will see the all glory of His creation as He meant us to see it, in His radiance. Indeed, we will see the actual face of God! How I long for that moment.

July 18, 2019

THE REALITY OF GRACE

But go, tell His disciples and Peter.

—Mark 16:7 (NASB)

The American baseball player Yogi Berra is famous for his malapropisms—phrases that don't seem to make any sense. But one of his quotes may be among the most profound things I've ever heard from a mortal. He is said to have remarked, "If I hadn't believed it, I'd have never seen it!" Just like grace; it must be believed to be experienced.

I've always thought of myself as a lot like the pre-Pentecost Peter: I often feel the need to speak before I've thought, to act before I've considered the action. And often, like Peter, I'm incredibly hard-headed and clueless. I'm reminded of Peter's actions at the Transfiguration, when we're told in Matthew 17, Mark 9 and Luke 9 that when Moses and Elijah had appeared there with Jesus, "Peter said to Jesus, 'Lord, it is good for us to be here; if You wish, I will make three tabernacles here, one for You, and one for Moses, and one for Elijah'" (Matthew 17:4 NASB)—not realizing what he was saying.

And like Peter, I've too often disappointed myself even more than anyone else when I've done something I've sworn I would never do. In Gethsemane, Peter along with James and John could not stay awake and pray as Jesus had asked. Instead, three times they fell asleep. All of us know of Jesus's warning to Peter that before the rooster would crow twice, Peter would deny Jesus three times, just as he did.

Aren't we so much like that? We read and we tout ourselves as humble servants. But then we follow our own paths, our own fears, our own ways. But the incredible truth of grace comes home in this passage, maybe my favorite in the scriptures—my favorite, possibly because I need to hear it over and over to really believe it.

Remember that incredible passage in Mark 16.

> When the Sabbath was over, Mary Magdalene, and Mary the mother of James, and Salome, bought spices, so that they might come and anoint Him. Very early on the first day of the week, they came to the tomb when the sun had risen. They were saying to one another, "Who will roll away the stone for us from the entrance of the tomb?" Looking up, they saw that the stone had been rolled away, although it was extremely large. Entering the tomb, they saw a young man sitting at the right, wearing a white robe; and they were amazed. And he said to them, "Do not be amazed; you are looking for Jesus the Nazarene, who has been crucified. He has risen; He is not here; behold, *here is* the place where they laid Him. *But go, tell His disciples and Peter, 'He is going*

ahead of you to Galilee; there you will see Him, just as He told you [emphasis mine]. They went out and fled from the tomb, for trembling and astonishment had gripped them; and they said nothing to anyone, for they were afraid.

—Mark 16:1-8 NASB

This is, without a doubt, the most profound expression of grace that I know. Peter was feeling ashamed, knowing that he'd denied his Lord and Master, knowing that he had shamed himself beyond redemption, knowing that he was not worthy as the Master's friend. But the angel's words were clear, and I believe deeply that these words were meant to cry out to every one of us the true depth of His grace: "Go tell His disciples *and Peter* [emphasis mine] (Mark 16:7 NASB)." There is no doubt those two words changed Peter, saved Peter. So in Acts 15:11 NASB when Peter says, "But we believe that we are saved through the grace of the Lord Jesus, in the same way as they also are." We know how deeply he feels this.

And the message of Mark 16:7 is clear to me. You see, I insert my name in that passage. "But go, tell the disciples *and Michael.*" His grace, His matchless love, and promise of redemption extends not only to a fallen disciple like Peter, but also to me, and to you. Say it aloud with me, inserting your name: "But go, tell the disciples and _____" (Mark 16:1–8 NASB).

Amazing grace, for Peter, for you, and for me. Only by the blood of Christ Jesus.

April 4, 2015

THE CHRISTMAS STAR

The Christmas story. We've all heard from the passages in Matthew and Luke of the story of Jesus's birth. But there's one part of the story that always leads to more questions.

According to the Gospel of Matthew, the star of Bethlehem revealed the birth of Jesus to the Magi. The star led them to Jesus where they worshiped him and gave him gifts. Many see the star as a miraculous sign to mark the birth of the Christ. Some claim that the star fulfilled a prophecy from Numbers: "There shall come a Star out of Jacob" (Numbers 24:17 KJV).

I think that there's something far more meaningful about the star. Isaiah 9:2 states it clearly: "The people walking in darkness have seen a great light; on those living in the land of deep darkness a light has dawned" (Isaiah 9:2 NIV).

The contrast between darkness and light is found over and over in the scriptures, but most prominently in the New Testament. But let's get a bit semantic here to find real meaning. The Oxford Dictionary defines *light* as "the natural agent that stimulates sight and makes things visible." It is the agent that allows us to see clearly. But darkness is not an agent. Instead, it is the absence of light, the absence of visibility. So wherever there is light, there can be no darkness. And wherever there is darkness, light will come to illuminate and make visible.

How perfect! Mankind had been in a state of darkness until the light came into the world to make things visible. And the star was the sign of that new light of the world! With that sign, no longer could anything stay invisible. Indeed, the message of the Gospel is that "where there is light, there can be no darkness at all" (1 John 1:5 NASB). And Jesus Christ was the light of the world, and at His birth that light shone brightly. Neither the schemes of kings nor despots nor governments, or as Paul says, "Neither death, nor life, nor angels, nor principalities, nor things present, nor things to come" (Romans 8:38 NASB) can put out that light, no matter how hard they try. That light has never been even slightly dimmed. It shines brightly to illuminate and make visible the world. Even His death could not dim the light, for He is risen, and His light shines brighter than ever! And it will continue to shine to eternity.

So the star represents God's promise to us: the light of the world is ours, and to borrow from C. S. Lewis, "No darkness can ever infect our light."

December 2015

MY PLANS, HIS PLANS

Many are the plans in a person's heart, but it is the LORD's purpose that prevails. —PROVERBS 19:21 NIV

I'm flying out of Portland, Maine, this morning, having driven down the beautiful coast from Rockland, Maine. I'm still chuckling over a sign I saw in front of a church just outside of Wiscassett. It said, "Want to see God laugh? Tell him your plans!"

How I can relate to that! And how even King David could relate. We are reminded over and over in scripture that our ways are not His ways and that we cannot know His ways.

So many times I've made plans for my life, intricate and exacting plans. Worked out the whole roadmap! But then something came along to derail even my best work. God saying, "Not so fast, My son." And what never ceases to cause me wonder is just *how* these things happen. I look back now and realize that, had my plans gone ahead, I would have tripped and fallen many times. But even though I trip and fall anyway, He's there to pick me back up.

The first two lines that David wrote in Psalm 23 are really the essence of God's relationship with us—with me. "The Lord is my shepherd; I shall not want" (Psalm 23:1 NASB). First of all, He is the good shepherd, watching over every need of His sheep. Shepherds don't have an easy job. Their job is seemingly never done, because of the character of their charges. I've never been around sheep, but my reading tells me that they are among the most dependent, needy animals on earth. They aren't very intelligent, and they get themselves in trouble too frequently. Sound familiar? If our Lord is our shepherd, watching over and protecting us, then the analogy must mean that we are like sheep. Hmm, troubling to say the least. Am I that dumb, that dependent, that needy? Oh, yeah. I am.

But then comes the second part of that verse. David says that we have not needs outside the shepherd. The shepherd makes certain his sheep have food, water, shelter when needed, and a path on which to walk. Isn't that exactly what our Shepherd has provided? And hasn't he provided even more? He gave created food to nourish bodies, and we eat. He gave us water to quench our thirst, so we drink. He has given His word as a path to Him. And hasn't He given us so much more? But—and here's where the analogy to sheep really hurts—we too often don't partake of that which He so freely has given. Too often we have our own plans. And so, how does that work out for us?

March 2015

ANOTHER DIMENSION

He has told us that His name is I Am. Yes, present tense. That's to tell us that He is. He is present with us always. He was before time began, and He will be. Confusing? No doubt it is, but I think that there's another reason why He told us His name. You see, I think that our perception of time is something He created for us, a dimension that is useful to us so that we can measure things. But what we perceive as a dimension is not a dimension, a limitation in the heavenly places.

My wife tells me that I'm obsessed with time. I like watches, and I love my phone. They are never far, and they tell me the time to the minute and second. I'm preternaturally early, because I want to be "on time." I know what time I went to bed last night and what time I arose this morning. Because my world seems to have always revolved around time. As a child, I wondered how in the world that God could be listening to my bedtime prayers and the bedtime prayers of hundreds of millions of children just like me all at the same time. Incomprehensible for a child. Maybe even more so for adults. When I was five, I wanted to be six, and on and on. When I entered college, I wanted to move on to medical school. Time defined my years of training. And then I entered into a practice where every day revolved around a schedule of appointment times. My travels are built around flight schedules and being "on time." Now as I'm in that season of life known as retirement, I find it so difficult to not be governed by time! As the writer of Ecclesiastes said,

> There is an appointed time for everything. And there is a time for every event under heaven—A time to give birth and a time to die;
> A time to plant and a time to uproot what is planted.
> A time to kill and a time to heal;
> A time to tear down and a time to build up.
> A time to weep and a time to laugh;
> A time to mourn and a time to dance.
> A time to throw stones and a time to gather stones;
> A time to embrace and a time to shun embracing.
> A time to search and a time to give up as lost;
> A time to keep and a time to throw away.
> A time to tear apart and a time to sew together;
> A time to be silent and a time to speak.
> A time to love and a time to hate;
> A time for war and a time for peace.
>
> —Ecclesiastes 3:1-8 NASB

But we're given clues throughout Scripture about God's view of time. Peter told us, "But do not let this one fact escape your notice, beloved, that with the Lord one day is like a thousand years, and a thousand years like one day" (2 Peter 3:8 NASB).

October 2016

THE REAL ROAD NOT TAKEN

I am the way, and the truth and the light.

—John 14: 6 NASB

Robert Frost penned the poem "The Road Not Taken" in 1920, but centuries before him an Israelite king beat him to the idea. The Psalms hold many well-known and loved passages, but maybe the most quoted is Psalm 23. It's brief, only six verses, but those verses are filled with some of the most comforting words in all of scripture. They are prayed at the bedside of many in the last hours of life; and they bring comfort to grieving ones after.

But the picture the psalmist David paints is of a shepherd and his sheep. A leader and his followers. A protector and the protected.

Hmm. That's disconcerting, because I somehow have always wanted to be a leader, not a follower. And I'm represented by sheep! Really? I think Ray Stedman may have said it best:

It occurs to me that if Jehovah is to be our shepherd, then we have to begin by recognizing that we are sheep. I don't like that analogy, frankly, because I don't like sheep. I come by my dislike honestly. I used to raise sheep. In high school I was in the 4-H club, and I had a herd of sheep and goats. Now goats I can abide, because they may be obnoxious, but at least they're smart. Sheep are, beyond question, the most stupid animals on the face of the earth. They are dumb and they are dirty and they are timid and defenseless and helpless. Mine were always getting lost and hurt and snake-bitten. They literally do not know enough to come in out of the rain. I look back on my shepherding days with a great deal of disgust. Sheep are miserable creatures.[3]

Couldn't we have been dogs following their master? Maybe Labrador retrievers. They're beautiful and they follow—most of the time. But sheep? Why sheep?

The answer lies embarrassingly embedded in our culture's singular desire: we have always wanted to be leaders, not followers. Every minute of every day, I'm challenged to lead where I want to go, to handle things the way I want to handle them. I've spent many hours in "leadership" training; but I have never seen a "followership" course, have you? And every minute of every day, I recognize the absolute futility of that sentence, because I am as "miserable" as Stedman's sheep.

The easy road to travel is the one I choose for myself, making choices based on my desires, my opinions, my this, my that, all my, my, my! And then I find my miserable self more miserable than ever because of my choices. The most difficult road for me is the other one, to follow. But that's exactly what He's told me, that He will be my shepherd, to lead me, to provide for me, to protect me, and to see to my needs.

I choose to take the road less taken. It's difficult, and I frequently fail before I turn back and run to catch up to my shepherd. But He's assured me that He's always there, waiting for a lost and miserable sheep. That is, indeed, the *real* road not taken. And—with apologies to Robert Frost—for me that has, indeed, made all the difference.

May 2016

THE REMARKABLE "ALL"

Say to the righteous that it will go well with them.

—Isaiah 3:10 NASB

And we know that God causes all things to work together for good to those who love God, to those who are called according to His purpose.

—Romans 8:28 NASB

These verses promise us that it is well with the righteous, *always*; and God causes *all* things to work together for good. What assurance we have.

All means just that—all. Everything that happens to His children will be well. Not "some things" or "good things" or "those things." These verses assure us that everything is in His hands, under His control.

Julian of Norwich (1342–after 1416) wrote the earliest surviving book in the English language to be written by a woman, *Revelations of Divine Love*. In her revelation, she famously wrote, "All shall be well, and all shall be well, and all manner of thing shall be well."[4]

When we face a worldwide viral disease or any other natural disaster, a rogue government across the globe, or any other challenge to our lives, we can rest on the promises that for you and me, for "those who love God" (Romans 8:28 NASB), for "the righteous" (Isaiah 3:20 NASB), all shall be well. What else do we need?

April 14, 2020

REFERENCES

1   Dallas Willard, *Renewing the Christian Mind: Essays, Interviews, and Talks* (HarperOne, 2016).

2   C. S. Lewis, *Mere Christianity* (Harper Collins, 2001), 174–176.

3   Ray Stedman, *Authentic Christianity*, https://www.raystedman.org/daily-devotions/psalms/no-want).

4   Julian of Norwich, trans. Clifton Wolters, *Revelations of Divine Love* (Penguin, 1966).